HISTORY'S GREATEST DISASTERS

THE CHERNOBYL DISASTER

by Rebecca Rissman

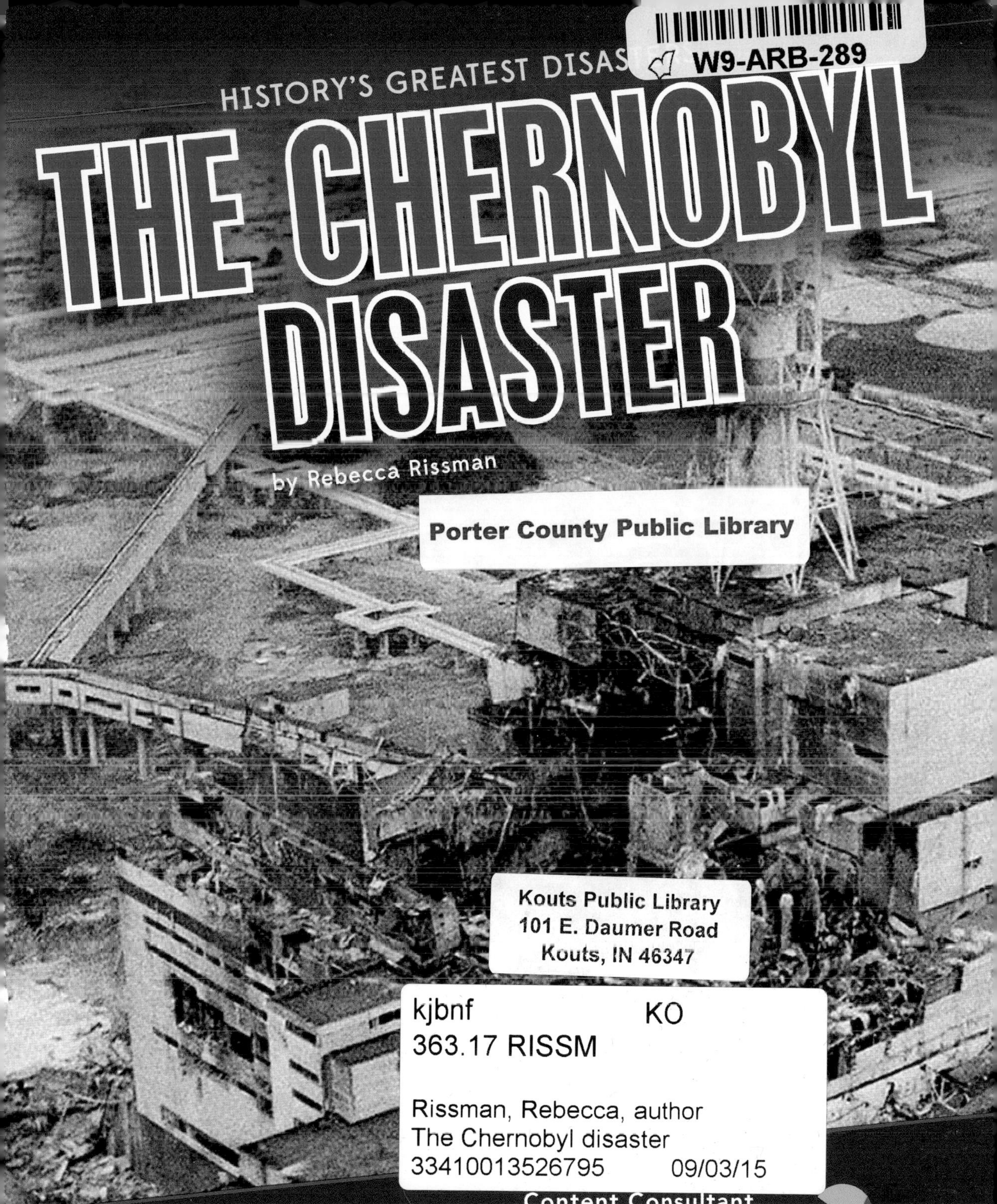

Content Consultant
Adriana Petryna
Professor, Department of Anthropology
University of Pennsylvania

CORE LIBRARY

Published by ABDO Publishing Company, PO Box 398166, Minneapolis, MN 55439. Copyright © 2014 by Abdo Consulting Group, Inc. International copyrights reserved in all countries. No part of this book may be reproduced in any form without written permission from the publisher. The Core Library™ is a trademark and logo of ABDO Publishing Company.

Printed in the United States of America,
North Mankato, Minnesota
042013
092013
♻ THIS BOOK CONTAINS AT LEAST 10% RECYCLED MATERIALS.

Editor: Jenna Gleisner
Series Designer: Becky Daum

Library of Congress Control Number: 2013932006

Cataloging-in-Publication Data
Rissman, Rebecca.
 The Chernobyl disaster / Rebecca Rissman.
  p. cm. -- (History's greatest disasters)
ISBN 978-1-61783-955-9 (lib. bdg.)
ISBN 978-1-62403-020-8 (pbk.)
Includes bibliographical references and index.
1. Chernobyl Nuclear Accident, Chernobyl, Ukraine, 1986--Juvenile literature. 2. Nuclear power plants--Accidents--Ukraine--Chernobyl--Juvenile literature.   I. Title.
363.17--dc23

                                        2013932006

Photo Credits: AP Images, cover, 1, 4, 24; iStockphoto, 7; Str/AP Images, 9; Red Line Editorial, 11, 23; Gamma-Rapho/Getty Images, 12; Sergei Supinsky/Getty Images, 15, 31; Rainer Klostermeier/str/AP Images, 18; Volodymyr Repik/AP Images, 22; Sergey Kamshylin/AP Images, 26, 34; Efrem Lukatsky/AP Images, 29, 41; Iryna Rasko/Shutterstock Images, 32, 45; Tomas Sereda/Shutterstock Images, 37; The Yomiuri Shimbun/AP Images, 39

CONTENTS

CHAPTER ONE

A TEST GOES WRONG

It was early on the morning of April 26, 1986. Employees at the Chernobyl Nuclear Power Plant in Ukraine lost control of an important safety test. A power surge sparked a giant explosion that tore through the roof of the plant. Just seconds later, the power plant caught fire. Flames shot into the sky. But the real disaster was only beginning.

The Chernobyl explosion of April 26, 1986, is considered history's greatest nuclear disaster.

The Chernobyl Nuclear Power Plant was leaking a dangerous and invisible material called radiation into the air. Radiation in large amounts is very harmful to living things. It can cause serious illness or even death. The amounts released by the Chernobyl power plant were hundreds of times stronger than what was considered safe. The radiation was about to become deadly.

The First Victims

The Chernobyl explosion killed two employees immediately. Another employee died of a heart attack shortly afterward. The smoke and raging fire carried the radiation up into the sky. Soon the wind carried

The town of Pripyat was built in 1970 to house the Chernobyl power plant workers and their families.

the radiation across the area. Radiation was detected as far as Japan.

Pripyat firefighters rushed to the plant to put out the enormous flames. Many were in such a hurry they did not even put on protective clothing. They wanted to put out the fire and save plant employees. These firefighters were the first to die of radiation sickness.

Residents in the town of Pripyat lived only two miles (3 km) from the power plant. They did not know they were being exposed to radiation. Nearly 30,000 people lived there. They did not feel, taste, or smell anything unusual yet.

The Chernobyl Nuclear Power Plant

The Chernobyl power plant created 10 percent of the energy used by Ukraine. In addition to energy, it also produced very large amounts of heat and radiation. This radiation had to be contained in order to stay safe. The employees at the plant knew creating nuclear power could be dangerous. The test they started running on April 25, 1986, was created to make sure they could control the plant if it lost power.

Many factors led to the disaster at Chernobyl. The machines used to make power were unstable. They overheated easily. Some people worried the walls could not keep radiation inside the plant if anything went wrong. Some of the employees in charge of the test were poorly trained. Some did not know the correct safety rules to follow.

An engineer inspects the damage in a machine room at the Chernobyl Nuclear Power Plant.

Nuclear Power

At the time of the disaster, nuclear power was a new and exciting source of energy. Scientists started experimenting with nuclear power as an electricity source in the 1950s. They had discovered that splitting atoms, or extremely small particles, could create energy or nuclear power. By the mid-1970s, nuclear power plants were making energy throughout North America, the former Union of Soviet Socialist

Republics (USSR), and Europe. The Chernobyl Nuclear Power Plant was up and running in May 1977.

Nuclear Power in History

The world learned about nuclear power in 1945. The United States dropped two atomic bombs that used nuclear power on Hiroshima and Nagasaki, Japan, to end World War II (1939-1945). The bombs were incredibly powerful and killed approximately 140,000 Japanese people. After World War II, scientists focused on using nuclear energy to create power for electricity and military purposes. The first nuclear power plant opened outside of Moscow, Russia, on June 27, 1954.

Scientists knew the radiation made at nuclear plants had to be handled carefully. It needed to be kept away from living things. It could not escape into the air. It could not seep into water sources such as rivers. Objects exposed to large amounts of radiation could become radioactive and spread radiation themselves.

Some people were afraid to have a nuclear power plant built near their homes or cities. People wondered what

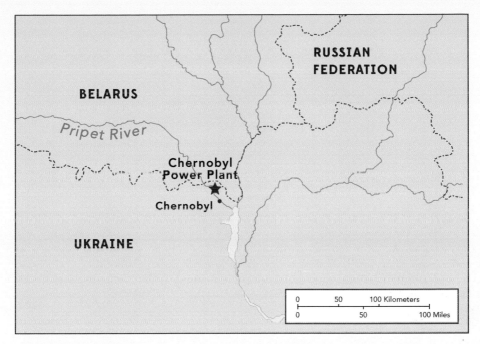

Chernobyl Area
This map shows the location of the Chernobyl Nuclear Power Plant. After reading about how unstable this type of plant was, do you think placing it near water sources and a populated area was a good idea?

would happen if workers lost control of a nuclear power plant. On March 28, 1979, there was an accident at the Three Mile Island Nuclear Generating Station in Pennsylvania. The accident caused very small amounts of radiation to leak into the air. No one was hurt by the radiation from this event. But it reminded people that a large disaster could release deadly amounts of radiation.

CHAPTER TWO

UNKNOWN DANGERS

The disaster at Chernobyl released 400 times the amount of radiation as one of the atomic bombs dropped on Japan. But people at the time did not understand how dangerous the situation was. Most of the machines used to measure radiation levels had been destroyed in the accident. The ones that remained no longer worked.

Even days after the explosion, workers and residents of Pripyat were not yet aware how deadly the radiation levels were.

Brave Divers

Radioactive water also built up inside the plant. If the levels of radiation in the water grew too high, there would have been an even bigger explosion. Two plant employees swam through the radioactive water to open vents and lower the levels. Their actions prevented an even bigger disaster and saved many lives. But they also exposed themselves to extremely high levels of radiation in the water.

Firefighters Respond

Firefighters arrived at the destroyed plant minutes after the explosion. Many crawled onto the roofs of the burning buildings of the plant. Others worked inside the damaged buildings. They worked hard for nearly five hours to put out other fires burning around the explosion site.

Within two hours, some of the firefighters felt very ill. Some said they could taste metal in the air. Others said their faces felt like they were being stuck by pins and needles. They did not know it yet, but they were suffering from radiation sickness.

Every year relatives and tourists visit this memorial in Ukraine to pay respect to the firefighters who fought the Chernobyl fire.

The View from Pripyat

Residents of Pripyat watched the cloud of radioactive smoke rise into the sky. They did not know they were in danger. Finally on April 27, the USSR government began to realize how serious the explosion had been. But the government did not tell the citizens of Pripyat the whole truth. Citizens were told that a small accident had occurred at the plant, and they would need to evacuate the area for three days. People packed small bags and left. They thought they would be back home soon. Sadly the residents would never be allowed to return. Their homes were far too radioactive to be safe.

Doctors and Nurses in Danger

Doctors and nurses in Kiev and Moscow weren't just worried about the first victims of the explosion. They were also worried that the patients were radioactive. The patients had been exposed to so much radiation that they could make others sick. Hospital employees wore special masks, boots, and gowns to protect themselves.

Treatment

Many plant workers and firefighters were rushed to hospitals. They had early signs of radiation sickness, which included vomiting and burns on their skin. Some were too sick for doctors to save. Others stayed in the hospital and battled health issues for months and even years.

Svetlana Alexievich, the wife of one of the sickened firefighters, wrote about the evacuation out of Pripyat:

> It's night. On one side of the street there are buses, hundreds of buses, they're already preparing the town for evacuation, and on the other side, hundreds of fire trucks. . . . Over the radio they tell us they might evacuate the city for three to five days, take your warm clothes with you, you'll be living in the forest. In tents. People were even glad—a camping trip! We'll celebrate May Day like that, a break from routine. People got barbeques ready. They took their guitars with them, their radios. Only the women whose husbands had been at the reactor were crying.
>
> Source: Svetlana Alexievich. Voices from Chernobyl. London: Dalkey Archive Press, 2005. Print. 8.

What's the Big Idea?

What is the author of this quote saying about the attitudes of people in Pripyat right after the accident? Why do you think people reacted to the evacuation the way they did? What details support her point?

THE WORLD LEARNS ABOUT CHERNOBYL

At 9:00 a.m. on April 28, high levels of radiation were detected in Finland, Sweden, Denmark, and Norway. USSR officials denied anything had happened at the Chernobyl power plant. People around the world worried about where the radiation was coming from.

Finally at 9:00 p.m. the USSR admitted there had been an accident. A news report in Moscow said one

A trash collector in Berlin, Germany, dumps vegetables contaminated by Chernobyl's radiation.

of the reactors at the Chernobyl power plant was damaged. But the report said there would not be any consequences from it. The report was misleading. It did not explain how dangerous the situation was. The fire inside the nuclear power plant was still burning and sending radiation into the air. Many firefighters and plant workers were already very ill with radiation sickness.

Liquidators

It took workers ten days to put out the fire burning inside the power plant. Helicopters dropped sand and chemicals onto the flames to help smother them. But the cleanup effort had just begun. The plant was still leaking radiation into the air.

Construction workers, plant employees, soldiers, miners, and volunteers worked to clean up the site and slow the spread of radiation. The government called these people liquidators because they were working to liquidate, or erase, the problems caused by the disaster at Chernobyl. At its busiest, there were 600,000 liquidators working on the plant. Many were not given clothing to protect them from the radiation at the plant. Many suffered radiation sickness in later years.

Exclusion Zone

In the weeks after the disaster, scientists in the USSR started to admit how terrible the radiation exposure near Chernobyl was. On May 14, 1986, the government called for an exclusion zone. Everyone living within

Sarcophagus

One of the biggest tasks for the liquidators was building a giant shell around the destroyed plant. It was called the sarcophagus. It kept radiation from leaking out into the air. The liquidators hurried to build it.

Liquidators who built the sarcophagus hold a sign reading, "We will fulfill the government's order!"

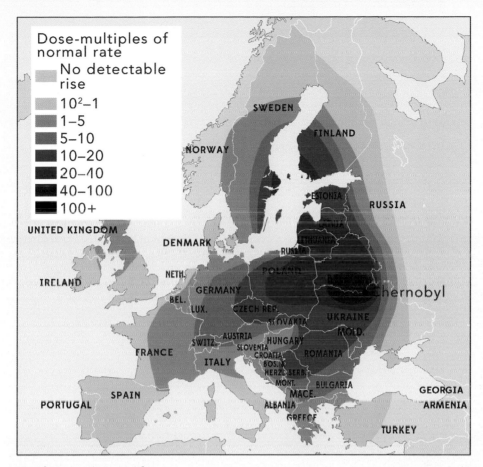

Radiation Levels

This map shows how radiation levels were multiplied throughout Europe one week after the Chernobyl disaster. How do you think people in Europe felt about the way the government first told them about the disaster? Should governments facing disasters like Chernobyl tell their citizens the truth?

20 miles (32 km) of the plant was forced to leave. Plants, animals, water, and land in this area had been affected by too much radiation and would harm people living there.

British newspaper headlines were covered with news of the Chernobyl Nuclear Power Plant disaster.

Radiation Spreads in the Wind

Wind carried clouds of radiation from Chernobyl into the rest of Ukraine, Russia, and Belarus. Within weeks smaller amounts were found in Northern Europe and North America. Scientists in the United States noticed radiation in the environment in early May 1986.

Most people living in countries affected by the radiation from Chernobyl were not harmed. Only those who were very close to the explosion site or those who had consumed items poisoned with radiation became ill. These people often felt sick for months or even years.

FURTHER EVIDENCE

Chapter Three discusses the effects of the radiation released by the Chernobyl power plant. What is the main point of this chapter? What details support this main point? Visit the Web site below to read more about the effects of radiation. Pick a fact or quote from the Web site that relates to the information in this chapter. How does this fact or quote support this chapter?

Radiation Sickness
www.mycorelibrary.com/chernobyl

CHAPTER FOUR

DISASTER CONSEQUENCES

In the first three months after the disaster, 28 firefighters and plant workers died of radiation sickness. Thousands of liquidators were hospitalized for their injuries. The final number of people who became sick or died because of the accident is unknown. The USSR released very little information about the accident. This made it difficult for scientists to count the number of sicknesses and deaths.

The city of Pripyat has since been abandoned. The levels of radiation in the area are still unsafe.

Today scientists estimate approximately 4,000 to 200,000 people who were near the plant during or right after explosion will die of cancers caused by the radiation. Most experts agree that many more will develop cancers or blood diseases.

Some groups of people suffered more than others. Pripyat residents who experienced high levels of radiation were badly affected. Many children living near the plant drank milk that had been exposed to radiation. Some of them developed cancer. The liquidators, plant workers, and firefighters suffered the most health issues. They had been exposed to much more radiation than other residents of the area.

Different Numbers

Scientists have trouble identifying the number of people who became sick or died because of this disaster. Radiation levels of the people who worked to clean up the disaster were very poorly monitored. And it is difficult to know if all sickness in Chernobyl was caused by radiation or not. But scientists are researching this question.

Some pine tree forests near Chernobyl died after the explosion, but they now grow in the area again.

Animals and Plants

The animals living near the power plant also suffered. Some pets and farm animals were evacuated from the exclusion zone. Others were left behind, and many became ill. Some animals that stayed in the zone got very sick, stopped reproducing, and even died.

The first wave of radiation killed many nearby trees, but most of the plants around the area continued to grow. Many of these plants have radiation inside them. People should not eat fruit or vegetables grown in the exclusion zone because they are often radioactive. Scientists worry that a forest fire could occur in this area. If the plants catch fire, the smoke would release radiation into the air.

Safety in the Zone

Today many people work in the exclusion zone. Some are still cleaning up radioactive trash. Others are busy building the new sarcophagus over the nuclear power plant. It will safely contain radiation and will last

Construction of a massive steel structure to contain the old sarcophagus and keep radiation inside began in 2010.

100 years. These workers do not stay in the exclusion zone for long. They wear protective clothing and carefully measure the radiation where they work.

Lasting Effects

People are still not allowed to live inside the exclusion zone. The levels of radiation in the plants, buildings, and soil are unsafe. The residents of Pripyat are allowed to visit once a year to see their relatives'

Many of the buildings in Pripyat, including this school, have been abandoned.

graves. Radiation lasts for a very long time. As time passes, the area around Chernobyl will get safer. But traces of radiation will remain in the area for approximately the next 48,000 years.

Some tourists visit the area. They tour the abandoned city of Pripyat. Buses drive them to the destroyed plant. But they are told they should not stay for long. They are also warned not to eat or drink anything from the area.

This quote comes from a soldier who worked as a liquidator after the disaster:

> *I went. I didn't have to go. I volunteered. . . .We came home. I took off all the clothes that I'd worn there and threw them down the trash chute. I gave my cap to my little son. He really wanted it. And he wore it all the time. Two years later they gave him a diagnosis: a tumor in his brain.*
>
> Source: Alexievich, Svetlana. Voices from Chernobyl. *London: Dalkey Archive Press, 2005. Print. 40.*

Changing Minds

In this quote, the soldier talks about the deadly effects radiation from his clothing had on his young son. How might he have reacted differently that day if he had known about the dangers of radiation contamination? Do you think he would have volunteered to be a liquidator?

CHAPTER FIVE

LEARNING FROM CHERNOBYL

Many of the mistakes made at Chernobyl have led to better rules for nuclear power plant safety. Today there are more than 400 nuclear power plants around the world.

Many steps have been taken to make sure a similar disaster cannot happen again. Employees at nuclear power plants are carefully trained to operate machines and keep radiation safely contained.

This monument was built in 2006, 20 years after the Chernobyl explosion. It stands outside the closed nuclear power plant to honor those lost in the disaster.

Why Nuclear Power?

Traditionally people have burned fossil fuels, such as coal and oil, to create power. These methods are expensive and do not produce very much power. They also use up limited resources and pollute the environment. Nuclear power can be less expensive, and it produces great amounts of power. When generated the correct way, nuclear power can be safer and less polluting to the environment.

Nuclear power plants are supposed to hold radiation inside the plant in case of an accident.

New rules have been made to make sure nuclear disasters cannot be kept secret. If an accident occurs at a nuclear power plant in the United States, it must be announced within 15 minutes so people can evacuate quickly.

Fukushima, Japan

On March 11, 2011, a large earthquake damaged the Fukushima Nuclear Power Plant in Japan. The Fukushima disaster released less than 1/10 of the radiation released during and after the Chernobyl explosion. This is because the Fukushima Nuclear

Nuclear power plants around the world provide energy to 31 countries.

Power Plant was built more safely than the Chernobyl Nuclear Power Plant. Strong structures were built around the machines that created nuclear power. They kept most of the radiation from leaking out after the disaster. Fukushima also used a much more stable method for making power. The Fukushima employees were better educated about nuclear power and radiation. They responded to the disaster quickly to reduce the threat.

How was Fukushima Different?

Three separate parts of the Fukushima Nuclear Power Plant in Japan were severely damaged. They released radiation but not as much as the Chernobyl disaster. The Fukushima plant was overwhelmed by seawater, which caused its backup generator to stop working.

Chernobyl's Legacy

The disaster at Chernobyl led to safer nuclear power plants. It also reminded some people about nuclear energy dangers. Today people still argue whether we should use nuclear power plants to

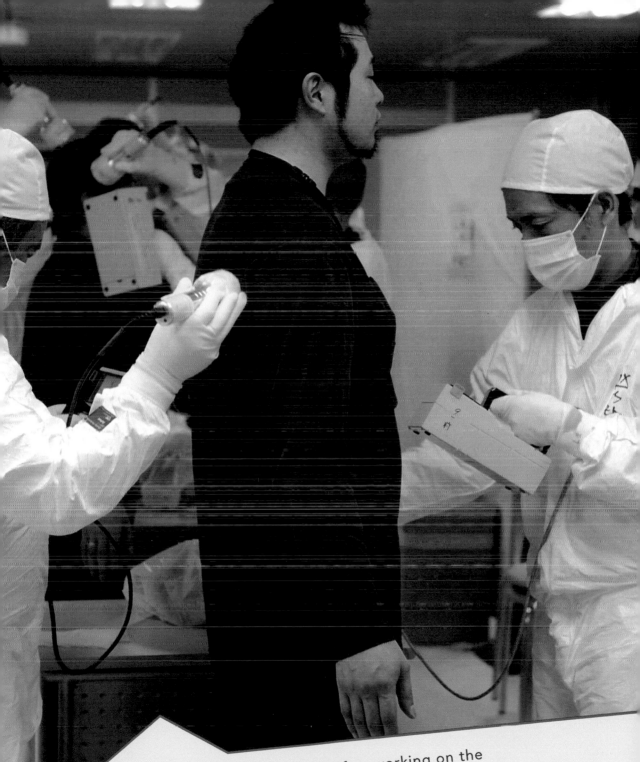

A man is tested for radiation after working on the Fukushima Nuclear Power Plant.

produce energy. The Chernobyl explosion will be remembered as the worst nuclear disaster in history. But it will also serve as a lesson to make nuclear plants safer in the future.

EXPLORE ONLINE

This book discusses the safety concerns and environmental impact of the Chernobyl Nuclear Power Plant disaster. Today nuclear power plants are much safer. But some people still worry about the risks of nuclear energy. Visit the Web site below to learn more about nuclear power and the environment. Do you think nuclear power is a good way to produce energy?

Nuclear Power and the Environment
www.mycorelibrary.com/chernobyl

A woman sets flowers next to a relative's picture near a monument in Kiev, Ukraine.

IMPORTANT DATES

1954

The world's first nuclear power plant opens near Moscow, Russia, on June 27.

1970

Construction of the Chernobyl Nuclear Power Plant begins. The city of Pripyat is founded.

1977

The Chernobyl Nuclear Power Plant becomes operational in May.

1986

The citizens of Pripyat are evacuated on April 27.

1986

Radiation is detected in Finland, Sweden, Denmark, and Norway on April 28.

1986

Radiation from the Chernobyl disaster is detected in the United States in early May.

1979

An accident at Three Mile Island Nuclear Generating Station in Pennsylvania leaks small amounts of radiation on March 28.

1986

The scheduled test at the Chernobyl Nuclear Power Plant begins on April 25.

1986

The giant explosion at the Chernobyl Nuclear Power Plant claims three lives on April 26 and begins the Chernobyl disaster.

1986

The Chernobyl explosion and radiation effects kill 28 people between May and July.

2010

Construction of a new sarcophagus over the Chernobyl Nuclear Power Plant begins in September.

2011

An earthquake causes an accident at the Fukushima Nuclear Power Plant in Japan on March 11.

Why Do I Care?

The Chernobyl disaster happened more than 25 years ago. Most experts believe the only area still dangerous is within the exclusion zone around the plant. So why does this story matter to you? What do you think about the dangers of radiation?

Take a Stand

This book discusses the positive and negative effects of nuclear energy. How do you feel about it? Make a list of all the positive things about nuclear energy. Then make a list of all the negative things. Once you've decided which side you stand on, write 200 words describing your opinion.

Say What?

Reading about nuclear energy can mean learning new vocabulary. Find four or five words in this book you have never seen or heard before. Use a dictionary to find their definitions. Then rewrite the definitions in your own words. Use each word in a new sentence.

Tell the Tale

Chapter Two discusses the evacuation of Pripyat. Imagine you lived in Pripyat and were forced to evacuate after the Chernobyl power plant explosion. Write a short story about your experience. What do you think about the evacuation? Are you worried about radiation?

GLOSSARY

atom
the smallest part of an element; nuclear power is created from splitting atoms into two to make energy.

evacuate
to leave an area under orders

exclusion zone
the area around the Chernobyl plant that is too dangerous for people to live within

expose
to come in contact with something

fossil fuels
natural fuel, such as coal or gas

liquidators
the group of workers hired by the USSR government to clean up the Chernobyl disaster site

nuclear power
power that comes from splitting atoms

radiation
invisible material created alongside nuclear power

radioactive
something that gives off radiation

sarcophagus
the structure built around the Chernobyl plant to contain radiation

LEARN MORE

Books

Greeley, August. *Fallout: Nuclear Disasters in Our World*. New York: PowerKids Press, 2003.

Lusted, Marcia Amidon. *The Chernobyl Disaster*. Edina, MN: ABDO, 2011.

Parker, Vic. *Chernobyl 1986: An Explosion at a Nuclear Power Station*. Chicago: Raintree, 2006.

Web Links

To learn more about the Chernobyl disaster, visit ABDO Publishing Company online at **www.abdopublishing.com**. Web sites about the Chernobyl disaster are featured on our Book Links page. These links are routinely monitored and updated to provide the most current information available.

Visit **www.mycorelibrary.com** for free additional tools for teachers and students.

INDEX

ABOUT THE AUTHOR

Rebecca Rissman is an award-winning children's nonfiction author and editor. She has written more than 100 books about history, science, and art. She lives in Portland, Oregon, with her husband and enjoys hiking, yoga, and cooking.